DATE DUE			

The Palestinian Conflict

Identifying Propaganda Techniques

Curriculum Consultant: JoAnne Buggey, Ph.D.
College of Education, University of Minnesota

By Neal Bernards

Greenhaven Press, Inc.
Post Office Box 289009
San Diego, CA 92198-0009

Titles in the opposing viewpoints juniors series:

AIDS	The Palestinian Conflict
Alcohol	Patriotism
Animal Rights	Poverty
Death Penalty	Prisons
Drugs and Sports	Smoking
The Environment	Television
Gun Control	Toxic Wastes
The Homeless	The U.S. Constitution
Immigration	Working Mothers
Nuclear Power	Zoos

Library of Congress Cataloging-in-Publication Data

Bernards, Neal, 1963–
    The Palestinian conflict: identifying propaganda techniques / by
Neal Bernards; curriculum consultant, JoAnne Buggey.
        p.   cm. — (Opposing viewpoints juniors)
    Summary: Eight articles debate the Palestinian/Israeli conflict,
focusing on the Palestinian right to a homeland, the treatment of
Palestinians by the Israelis, the role of the United States in the
conflict, and if peace is possible.
    ISBN 0-89908-602-0
    1. Jewish-Arab relations—Juvenile literature.   2. Israel-Arab
conflicts—Juvenile literature.   3. Palestinian Arabs—
Juvenile literature.   4. Critical thinking—Juvenile literature.
[1. Jewish-Arab relations—1973–   2. Israel-Arab conflicts.
3. Palestinian Arabs.   4. Critical thinking.]   I. Buggey, JoAnne.
II. Title. III. Series.
DS119.7.B42   1990
95604—dc20   90-37741
                                                      CIP
                                                      AC

Cover photo: Wide World Photos

CONTENTS

An Introduction to
Opposing Viewpoints

When people disagree, it is hard to figure out who is right. You may decide one person is right just because the person is your friend or a relative. But this is not a very good reason to agree or disagree with someone. It is better if you try to understand why these people disagree. On what main points do they differ? Read or listen to each person's argument carefully. Separate the facts and opinions that each person presents. Finally, decide which argument best matches what you think. This process, examining an argument without emotion, is part of what critical thinking is all about.

This is not easy. Many things make it hard to understand and form opinions. People's values, ages, and experiences all influence the way they think. This is why learning to read and think critically is an invaluable skill. Opposing Viewpoints Juniors books will help

you learn and practice skills to improve your ability to read critically. By reading opposing views on an issue, you will become familiar with methods people use to attempt to convince you that their point of view is right. And you will learn to separate the authors' opinions from the facts they present.

Each Opposing Viewpoints Juniors book focuses on one critical thinking skill that will help you judge the views presented. Some of these skills are telling fact from opinion, recognizing propaganda techniques, and locating and analyzing the main idea. These skills will allow you to examine opposing viewpoints more easily. Each viewpoint in this book is paraphrased from the original to make it easier to read. The viewpoints are placed in a running debate and are always placed with the pro view first.

What Are Propaganda Techniques?

Propaganda is information presented in an attempt to influence people. In this Opposing Viewpoints Juniors book you will be asked to identify and study several common propaganda techniques. Some of these techniques appeal to your ability to think logically while others appeal to your emotions.

All propaganda techniques distract the listener or reader from the complete picture. People who use propaganda techniques encourage you to look only at the factors that are important to accepting their argument as true. The propaganda will be offered as a reason to believe the argument, but in reality will be weak, distracting, or irrelevant reasons.

It is important to learn to recognize these techniques, especially when reading and evaluating differing opinions. This is because people who feel strongly about an issue use many of these techniques when attempting to persuade others to agree with their opinion. Some of these persuasive techniques may be relevant to your decision to agree or not, but others will not be. It is important to sift through the information, weeding the proof from the false reasoning.

While there are many types of propaganda techniques, this book will focus on two of them. These are *testimonial* and *scare tactics*. Examples of these techniques are given below:

Testimonial—quoting or paraphrasing an authority or celebrity to support one's own argument. Often, the celebrity is not qualified to express an opinion on the subject. For example, movie stars are often used to recommend a product they may know nothing about. Bill Cosby, for example, will be used in a commercial to endorse a camera. But Cosby is an actor, not a photographer. The commercial is deceptive—it asks you to accept the advice of someone who is not a true authority on the topic.

Testimonials can be used in a positive way as well. If the person quoted is truly an authority on the subject being talked about, the testimonial can support an argument. Quoting comedian Richard Pryor about how drugs almost ruined his life is an example of a testimonial that presents a legitimate reason to believe drugs can be dangerous. Pryor *is* an authority on this subject and can give advice based on his personal experience.

Scare tactics—the threat that if you do not do or believe this, something terrible will happen. People using this technique write or say alarming words and phrases to persuade you to believe their argument.

An example is "illegal immigration endangers every worker in the United States." The person quoted does not say *how* illegal immigration will endanger everyone. The purpose of the statement is to scare you into believing his argument. The person wants you to make a decision based on fear about the issue, not on logical reasoning.

When reading differing arguments, then, there is a lot to think about. Are the authors giving sound reasons for their points of view? Or do they distort the importance of their arguments by using testimonials deceptively, or by playing on your fear and emotions through scare tactics?

We asked two students to give their opinions on the Palestinian conflict. Look for examples of testimonial and scare tactics in their arguments:

I think Israel should be reserved for Jews.

Last year in school we learned about the Holocaust. We learned that six million Jews were murdered during World War II. Our teacher told us that Hitler and his Nazi army killed Jews because they blamed them for Germany's problems. She also said it was not the first time in history Jews had been mistreated.

It seems that no matter where Jews live, they must deal with angry people. Jews need a place to live where they will not be murdered by ruthless enemies. Israel is a good country for this. According to the Bible, Jews and their ancestors lived in Israel for centuries. Since the Jews were in Israel first, I think they should be allowed to stay.

I think the Jews and the Palestinians should share Israel.

I have a friend named Fadia. Her parents left Palestine in 1967 when the Arabs and Israelis fought a war. Now the Israelis won't let Fadia or her parents back into the country. I don't think that's fair.

Fadia's family lived in Israel, or Palestine, as they call it, for hundreds of years. They farmed land along the Jordan river. Now Jewish settlers live there and say they will never give the land back. The settlers have lived there for only ten years, but they act like they've been there forever.

Fadia's parents grew up in Palestine. It's their home country. They told me that the Israeli army forced them to leave their farm in 1948. No one should be forced to leave the place where they grew up. Some Palestinians have used terrorism as a way to get their country back.

I think the Jews in Israel should allow Palestinians to live peacefully in Israel. Both groups have a right to live there.

ANALYZING THE
SAMPLE VIEWPOINTS

Benjamin and Sarah have very different ideas about who should be allowed to live in Israel. Both of them use propaganda techniques in their arguments:

Benjamin:

TESTIMONIAL

His teacher said that six million Jews were killed during the Holocaust because Hitler used them as scapegoats.

SCARE TACTIC

Jews need a homeland so that they will not be murdered.

Sarah:

TESTIMONIAL

Her friend Fadia's family told her that they were forced to leave their farm by the Israeli army.

SCARE TACTIC

Palestinians may use violence to get their land and country back.

In this sample, Benjamin and Sarah use some propaganda techniques when presenting their opinions. Both Benjamin and Sarah think they are right about who should live in Israel. What do you conclude about the problem from this sample? Why?

As you continue to read through the viewpoints in this book, try keeping a tally like the one above to compare the authors' arguments.

CHAPTER 1

PREFACE: Do the Palestinians Have a Right to a Homeland?

The problem between the Palestinians and the Israelis exists because both groups claim the same land. Four wars have been fought between Arabs and Jews over who should live in Israel. The Jews have won every war. In 1948, after the first war, the Jewish nation of Israel was established alongside the Arab nation of Palestine. Immediately after its creation, Israel was invaded by five other nations that attempted to destroy it. The Israelis fought back and defeated the other countries. During this war, called the War of Independence, thousands of Palestinians in Jewish portions of Israel were forced to leave their homes during the fighting. Most escaped to refugee camps in Palestine. However, in the Six-Day War of 1967, the Israeli army occupied the territory of Palestine. This occupied territory, now called the West Bank (it lies on the west bank of the Jordan River) and the Gaza Strip, has been managed by the Israeli government ever since.

Many people believe the way the Israelis treat the Palestinians in the occupied territories is unjust. Palestinians are not allowed the same rights as Israelis and often live in much poorer conditions. These people would like Israel to give back this land to the Palestinians. In this way, they believe, peace could be achieved, and both Israelis and Palestinians could have a "homeland."

Many Israelis and those who support them disagree. They argue that Israel justly won this land in war—a war, they add, they did not want. In addition, these supporters believe that returning this land would endanger Israel's security.

The next two viewpoints debate the issue of whether the Palestinians have a right to a homeland. In these viewpoints, you will find examples of testimonials and scare tactics.

The Palestinians have a right to a homeland

Editor's Note: From 1920 to 1948, England ruled Palestine. In the following viewpoint, the author argues that English rulers promised Palestinians a land of their own. He writes that this promise has not been kept. Watch for the propaganda techniques the author uses, especially scare tactics.

"Bloodshed" and "terrorism" are frightening words. What propaganda technique is this?

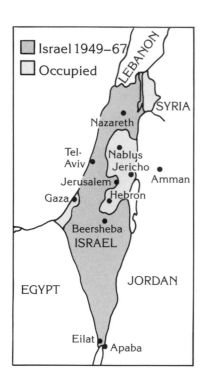

Israel 1949–67
Occupied

If there is to be peace in the Middle East, Israel must allow the Palestinians to have their own country. Nothing else will stop the bloodshed and terrorism. In 1948 the Jews got their own country. Now it is time for the Palestinians to get theirs.

For over seven hundred years, Arab people have lived in the land of Palestine, now called Israel. Jews did not begin to come to Palestine in great numbers until the beginning of this century. The Palestinians built villages, planted crops, and raised farm animals on this land. Israel had no right to take the land and destroy the villages in the wars of 1948 and 1967. Nor do they have a right to keep this land. Until it is given back, Palestinians will protest Israel's unjust rule of the West Bank and Gaza Strip.

In 1915 England promised to support Palestine as an independent state. The Palestinians of that time helped England fight Turkey during World War I. In return for the Palestinians' help, England promised that Palestine would become an Arab nation. That promise has not been kept. After studying the problem in 1939, Arab historian George Antonius wrote, "There is no valid reason why Palestine should not become an independent Arab state." Antonius thought that Jews and Palestinians could live together in one country. He was wrong.

In 1948 the United Nations divided Palestine into an Arab state and a Jewish state. A war started immediately. The Jews threw thousands of Palestinians out of the country and have not let them return. To this day, Palestinians live in dusty, overcrowded refugee camps in Gaza, the West Bank, and Lebanon. Each war after that forced more Palestinians into refugee camps.

Today, almost five million Palestinians are spread out across the world in countries like Jordan, Lebanon, West Germany, and the United States. These people need a place where they can live in peace and security. They need the right to vote, the right to own property, and the right to work wherever they want.

If any people should understand the Palestinians' desire to have a homeland, it is the Jews. The nationless Palestinians of today are like the European Jews of the 1930s. During World War II, no one protected the Jews from destruction at the hands of the Nazis. No nation claimed responsibility for the Jews. Now hundreds of Palestinian men, women, and children are being killed each year at the hands of Israeli soldiers. It is time to give Palestinians a chance to defend themselves and a chance to run their own lives. If they do not get this chance, the fighting will continue.

The author says that Palestinians are unsafe until they get their own country. Is this a scare tactic? Why or why not?

Nafez Nazzal is a Palestinian professor of Middle East history at Birzeit University near Jerusalem. He says that peace is impossible until Jews and Palestinians can live side by side. He wants Israel to return the occupied territories of the West Bank and Gaza Strip to the Palestinians. Nazzal argues that Palestinians will fight Israeli rule as long as the injustice continues. The occupied territories, he says, were considered Palestinian territory before the Six-Day War in 1967. Since this war, Israel has controlled the West Bank and Gaza Strip through violence and intimidation. Most of the deaths take place in the territories. If the West Bank and Gaza Strip were given to the Palestinians, peace would return to the Middle East.

What nationality is Nazzal? How might this affect his opinion?

Thousands of Israelis and Palestinians are hurt and killed each year during violent demonstrations calling for a Palestinian homeland. It is time Israel recognized the Palestinians' right to control their future. If Israel does not respond, the killings will go on.

Has the author proved that people will die if Palestine does not become a state? Why or why not?

The author writes that Palestinians will not be safe until they have a homeland. What evidence does he give to support this claim? Is this a propaganda technique? If so, which one?

The Palestinians do not have a right to a homeland

Editor's Note: In the following viewpoint, the author writes of a group called the Palestine Liberation Organization (PLO). The PLO has used terrorist tactics in its fight for a Palestinian state. Read the viewpoint carefully to see how the author uses propaganda techniques to support his argument.

Why is the suggestion that the U.S. return land won in wars a scare tactic?

At one time, the Palestinians did have a homeland. When the United Nations divided Palestine into Jewish and Arab sections, the Palestinians could have quietly accepted the solution. They did not. Instead, five Arab nations attacked the tiny Jewish nation of Israel and lost. If a country loses a war, it cannot demand anything. Palestinians were the losers. They gave up their right to a homeland. To believe otherwise is to believe that America should give its land back to England or to Native Americans.

PUPILS AND TEACHERS

	All Schools in West Bank/Gaza Strip Area					Government-run Schools				
	80/81 (a)		67/68		Rate of Increase	80/81 (a)		67/68		Rate of Increase
	Total	Rate	Total	Rate		Total	Rate	Total	Rate	
Pupils:	410,523	100%	222,266	100%	85%	269,617	100%	134,859	100%	101%
Boys	225,577	55%	130,675	59%	73%	151,882	56%	83,823	62%	81%
Girls	184,946	45%	91,591	41%	102%	117,735	44%	51,016	38%	131%

	80/81			67/68			Rate of Increase	
	Teachers	Pupils	Pupils per Teacher	Teachers	Pupils	Pupils per Teacher	Teachers	Pupils
Teachers:		(a) (b)						
All the areas	13,565(a)	410,328	30(a)	7,463	222,266	30	82%	85%
Judea-Samaria	9,287	266,426	29	5,316	142,216	27	75%	87%
Gaza district & northern Sinai	4,278(a)	143,902(a)	33(a)	2,147	80,050	37	99%	80%

(a) excluding El-Arish, transferred to Egypt in 1979
(b) excluding southern Sinai

SOURCE: Israeli Ministry of Defense.
*1967–1968 figures show the number of students enrolled in schools before Israeli occupation. 1980–1981 figures show improvement in enrollment figures after the occupation.

Jews worked hard to make Israel the prosperous country it is today. Former White House Middle East expert Joan Peters points out that Arabs moved into Palestine only after the Jewish pioneers came in the 1920s and 1930s. Claims that Palestinians have lived there for hundreds of years are exaggerated, she says. Palestinians, she states, have no more right to the land than do Jews. Before the Jews came, Palestine was a barren, swampy land barely habitable for humans. The Jewish workers on the kibbutzes, or communal farms, put in decades of back-breaking work to make the soil suitable for farming. It was Jewish, not Palestinian, labor that turned Israel into the productive country it is today.

As a matter of fact, says Yehuda Z. Blum, there never existed a place called "Palestine" before the British Mandate of 1920. Blum, a professor at the Hebrew University in Jerusalem, says the area called Palestine was ruled by distant countries until 1948. Since Palestine never existed as a nation, Palestinians can make no claim that their land was taken from them.

Where does Mr. Blum teach? How might that influence his opinion about Palestine?

A separate Palestinian state might one day destroy Israel. The four wars with Arab countries and countless terrorist attacks by Palestinians on Israeli citizens proves this point. It would be suicide for Israel to allow the creation of a hostile nation on its own border. During Israel's history, Palestine Liberation Organization (PLO) terrorists have regularly crossed the border to kill Israeli people. In 1974, eighteen people were killed by terrorists in the border town of Kiryat Shmona. A month later, other Palestinian terrorists took Israeli schoolchildren hostage in the Galilee town of Ma'alot. Twenty-two children died when the terrorists shot them after Israeli soldiers attacked. How can Israel possibly give into demands by people who kill like this?

The author implies that Palestinians want to kill Jews. What propaganda technique is this?

Many examples of terrorism are given. Are these examples scare tactics? Why or why not?

Palestinians can live safely within the West Bank and Gaza Strip. But Palestinians do not allow the Israelis to live in safety and peace. Palestinians demand the right to establish a nation that might someday destroy Israel. By their use of terrorism, Palestinians have proven that they cannot be trusted. Their demand for a Palestinian homeland should not be met.

Has the author proven that Palestinians cannot be trusted? Why or why not?

The author writes that the Jewish Israelis would be endangered by a Palestinian state. List some reasons he gives to support this argument. How are the arguments in the second viewpoint different from those in the first? Who do you believe is in more danger? Why?

CRITICAL THINKING SKILL 1

Identifying Propaganda Techniques

After reading the two viewpoints on the Palestinians' right to a homeland, make a chart similar to the one made for Sarah and Benjamin on page 8. List one example of each propaganda technique from each viewpoint. A chart is started for you below:

Viewpoint 1:

TESTIMONIALS

Arab historian George Antonius wrote, "There is no valid reason why Palestine should not become an independent Arab state."

Viewpoint 2:

SCARE TACTICS

A Palestinian state might one day destroy Israel.

After completing your chart, answer the following questions:
    Which article used the most propaganda techniques?
    Which argument was the most convincing? Why?

CHAPTER

PREFACE: Are the Palestinians Treated Fairly?

Since December 1987, Palestinians have violently protested Israel's presence on the West Bank and Gaza Strip. This protest is called the "intifada" in Arabic. During the intifada, Palestinian youths have attacked Israeli soldiers and raised illegal Palestinian flags. So far they have not used guns. But they throw rocks at Israeli army patrols. They also drop cement blocks on soldiers' heads from rooftops in the narrow, winding streets of Arab villages. Scores of soldiers have been hurt during Palestinian protests.

In reaction to these violent protests, the Israeli soldiers often beat and imprison the demonstrators and even shoot them with rubber bullets. They chase rock-throwing Palestinian children through the streets, beating them with wooden clubs if they catch them. The rubber bullets are used to break up crowds of rock-throwing Palestinians. These bullets, steel balls wrapped in a thin coat of plastic, cause large bruises, broken bones, and even death. Thousands of Palestinians have suffered broken bones and bruised bodies from the bullets and the beatings. Hundreds of less fortunate Palestinians have died.

Many people think the Palestinians are right to protest because they are treated unfairly. They argue that much of their farmland has been taken from them by Israelis during the various wars. Also, Palestinians cannot elect the officials who govern them in the West Bank and Gaza Strip. In addition, no Arab nation will accept Palestinians as citizens. So thousands of them still live in crowded, filthy refugee camps.

Israeli leaders and others claim that the Palestinians are treated fairly. They argue that Palestinian living conditions in the occupied territories have improved since 1967. Israelis contend that Palestinians get a better education, better health care, and better housing than they did under Arab rule. Palestinians should consider themselves fortunate to live in a nation where human rights are valued.

The Arab-Israeli conflict has been going on since Jewish emigrants began arriving in great numbers in the 1920s. Few people believe it will end soon. Because it is an emotional subject, arguments on both sides use many propaganda techniques. In the next two viewpoints, look for examples of testimonial and scare tactics.

Editor's Note: In the following viewpoint, the author argues that the Israeli government treats Palestinians better than the previous Arab rulers did. He believes the Palestinians should be thankful for the opportunities Israel provides. The author quotes several authorities to support his argument. Use your critical reading skills to analyze these testimonials.

Palestinians under Israeli rule should not complain. Israel treats them better than any other government has treated them, including Arab nations like Jordan and Egypt. In the occupied territories of the Gaza Strip and the West Bank, Palestinians receive excellent health care, free education, high-quality food, and job opportunities.

The author writes that Palestinian lives have improved in the last twenty years. What evidence does he give to support his argument?

In 1967, under Egyptian and Jordanian rule, the average life span for a Palestinian was forty-eight years. Now it is sixty-two years. The Israeli health-care system is responsible for this improvement. For example, epidemics that once wiped out hundreds of people are now under control. Clean running water flows through Palestinian villages. And the food Palestinians eat has improved.

PERCENTAGE OF HOUSEHOLDS CONTAINING THESE ITEMS BEFORE AND AFTER ISRAELI OCCUPATION				
	Gaza District		Judea/Samaria	
	1967	mid 1980s	1967	mid 1980s
Refrigerator	3%	77%	5%	60%
Washing Machine	3%	32%	5%	30%
Television	3%	78%	2%	67%
Cooking Oven	4%	37%	8%	27%
Cooking Range	3%	87%	5%	80%
Kitchen	56%	96%	45%	74%
Running Water	14%	51%	18%	45%
Bathtub	18%	44%	23%	35%
Electricity	18%	88%	23%	82%
Private Car	5%	14%	2%	10%

SOURCE: Israeli Information Centre

Israel also gives Palestinian children a good education. A 1986 report issued by the Israel Information Center says that the number of Palestinian adults who have attended school has increased by 50 percent since the early 1970s. Students in these schools study the same subjects as students in Jordan and Egypt. Israel does not force Palestinians to study Hebrew or Israeli culture. Once students finish high school, they can go to one of the five universities in the West Bank or Gaza district. Israel created these universities after they took control of the territories. Prior to 1967, when Jordan had control, no Palestinian universities existed. The Israelis have proven their desire to help Palestinians.

Who issued the report? How might that affect this testimonial?

Just as in centuries past, agriculture remains the Palestinians' main industry. But with Israeli help, Palestinian farms have become more efficient. A report from the Israel Information Center says that there are six times more tractors in the territories than in 1970. More farm machines mean more food. More food means cheaper prices and healthier diets for Palestinian families.

The greatest improvement, however, is in the Palestinians' ability to find work in Israel. A report by the Israeli Ministry of Labour and Social Affairs states, "This rapid growth [in Palestinian standard of living] has been stimulated by contact with the economy of Israel." About one out of every three Palestinians now works in Israel. This income allows them to live better than under Arab rule. Another advantage the Palestinians have is that they are able to live in a democratic society. Israel is a Western-style democracy like the United States. No Arab nation can make this claim. This means that Israel ensures certain basic human rights. Peter Schwartz, the editor of *The Intellectual Activist,* says, "The Arabs who are rioting against Israel do not seek freedom. Palestinians are in fact far freer even under the so-called occupation by Israel than they would be under any type of Arab government."

Do you think a Palestinian report might come to different conclusions? Why or why not?

The author gives little information about Mr. Schwartz. How does that hurt your ability to evaluate his testimonial?

Israel provides Palestinians with the right to live in a democracy and the opportunity to work and live in peace. Israel treats Palestinians fairly.

What evidence does the author give that Palestinians' lives have improved? Do you think the author supports his argument well? After reading this viewpoint, do you think Palestinians are treated fairly? Why or why not?

The author writes of violent police actions. What propaganda technique might he be using? Support your answer.

Palestinians will not be treated fairly until they are allowed to rule themselves. Under Israel's cruel occupation, Palestinians have no rights. Israel unfairly imprisons Palestinians, restricts their movements, beats their children, steals their land, and deports their leaders.

Entire Palestinian cities and villages can be placed under curfew by the Israeli army. Curfews are a common form of punishment after a violent Palestinian protest. An entire village can be punished for the actions of a few rock throwers. During curfews, Palestinians cannot leave their homes, go to work, or buy food. Sometimes Palestinians are under curfew all day. At other times it may be from sundown to sunrise. Refugee camps can be placed on curfew anywhere from one day to a few weeks.

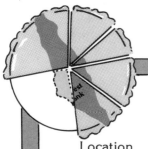

NUMBER OF SETTLEMENTS AND LAND CONFISCATED IN THE WEST BANK

Location	Land Confiscated (Dunams)	Number of Settlements	Number of Settlers	Number of Housing Units Already Estab.	Planned
Around Jerusalem	94,564	11	76,000	26,918	44,450
Ramallah and al-Bireh	35,600	12	1,514	198	50
Hebron, Bethlehem, and Jericho	116,150	12	6,895	543	8,000
Nablus, Jenin and Tulkarm	20,850	14	1,050	246	2,237
Jordan Valley	80,700	19	4,688	145	330
TOTAL	347,874	68	90,147	28,050	55,067

SOURCE: Mahdi Abd El-Hadi, "The Israeli Settlements in Jerusalem and the West Bank, 1967–1977," *Arab Thought Forum* (Jerusalem, May 1978), p. 61.

If protests continue in spite of the curfews, the army uses more severe measures. A common punishment is to blow up the homes of suspected Palestine Liberation Organization (PLO) leaders and of parents whose children get caught throwing stones at Israeli soldiers. Since Israeli occupation began, over 20,000 homes have been dynamited. There are no trials or chances to prove innocence. Sometimes the wrong houses are blown up.

The beatings of children caught throwing stones occur daily. Palestinian children are so badly beaten that their arms and hands are often broken. Soldiers often blindly rush into crowds of Palestinian children swinging their wooden batons. At other times they fire rubber bullets at rock-throwing children. These bullets have killed many innocent bystanders.

The attitude of Israeli soldiers is summed up by one young man who said, "I would like to see all the Palestinians dead because they are a sickness wherever they go." Many Israeli soldiers feel the same way. And it is these dangerous men who patrol Palestinian villages and towns.

Israelis also often steal Palestinian land. It is easy to do since Palestinians cannot return to Israel once they leave. If Palestinian landowners leave or get kicked out of the country, the Israeli government says they have given up the rights to their land. The land is then turned over to Orthodox Jewish settlers or other Israeli farmers. According to PLO representative Abdallah Frangi, 85 percent of all West Bank land on which Israelis live has been stolen from Palestinian farmers.

As a last measure, Israeli authorities can deport Palestinians they believe to be members of the PLO or intifada leaders. To deport someone means to force them to leave the country. Frangi says that since 1967 over two thousand Palestinians—mostly lawyers, teachers, doctors, and mayors—have been deported. These people are not dangerous terrorists. Israel deports them just to scare the Palestinians and make them obey.

Palestinians have no future in Israel. The world should not allow Israel to govern the territories any longer. Israel has never treated, and will never treat, Palestinians fairly.

The author writes of harsh measures to punish Palestinians. What propaganda technique is this?

Is this a scare tactic? Why or why not?

The author uses one quote from one soldier to support his point. Is this testimonial a propaganda technique?

Who does Mr. Frangi work for? How might this influence his opinion?

The author gives a frightening picture of Palestinian life under Israeli occupation. He tries to shock the reader with descriptions of terrible Israeli oppression. What propaganda technique is this? Do these graphic examples make the arguments more convincing? Why or why not?

2 Identifying Propaganda Techniques

This activity will allow you to practice identifying the propaganda techniques you have been learning in this book. The statements below focus on the subject matter of this chapter—whether or not Palestinians are treated fairly. Read each statement and consider it carefully. *Mark an S for any statement you believe is an example of scare tactics, T for any statement that is a testimonial, and N for a statement that is neither.*

If you are doing this activity as a member of a class or group, compare your answers with other class or group members. You may find that others have different answers from yours. Listening to the reasons others give for their answers can help you in identifying propaganda techniques.

EXAMPLE: A report by the Israel Information Center says that the number of Palestinian adults who have attended school increased by 50 percent.

ANSWER: T, testimonial. The author is using a report by an Israeli organization to support his argument.

Answer

1. Soldiers often rush into crowds of Palestinian children blindly swinging their wooden batons.   _____

2. The bloody wars between Jews and Arabs were fought in 1948, 1956, 1967, and 1973.   _____

3. Aban Eban, a prominent Israeli peace activist, says that Palestinians must receive fair treatment before peace can come about.   _____

4. Many Palestinians consider themselves to be like the persecuted Jews of old. Author Muhammad El-Farra writes that Palestinians have been unjustly forced into exile or into refugee camps.   _____

5. If ordinary citizens do not stop the bloodshed in Israel, they will all be responsible for the next violent war between Arabs and Jews.   _____

CHAPTER 3

PREFACE: What Role Should the U.S. Play in the Middle East?

In 1948, the United States became one of the first countries to recognize the new nation of Israel. The U.S. and Israel have had a close relationship ever since. Many people think it is too close.

To help the Israelis, the U.S. has given them three times more aid than it gives to all other Middle Eastern countries. Critics of the American-Israeli friendship dislike this. These critics want more U.S. money given to other Arab nations and less to Israel. They argue that Israel only uses this aid to build up its military, which keeps the war going. They believe peace might come if the U.S. helped poor Arab countries.

Supporters of Israel want the U.S. to give even more money to the Jewish state. They want Israel to remain a military powerhouse in the Middle East so that it can defend itself against its Arab neighbors. The majority of the six million Jews in America, along with many Christians, want to see the special relationship between the U.S. and Israel continue.

The following viewpoints debate the role the U.S. should play in the Middle East. The authors use many testimonials. Read the viewpoints carefully to see whether the testimonials help to make the arguments more convincing. Decide whether they are propaganda techniques.

What does the author say will happen if the U.S. does not aid Israel? Is this a scare tactic?

America has no better friend than the nation of Israel. Since joining the United Nations, Israel has voted for American interests 90 percent of the time. No other ally, including England or West Germany, can boast such a good voting record. Israel also gives America invaluable military information. Israelis test new American weapons and report how these weapons perform in battle. Israelis can also tell Americans which Arab armies are the strongest. If the U.S. abandoned Israel, America would be much more vulnerable to foreign attack.

Pat Crowley. Copley News Service. Reprinted with permission.

Israel's strong army also helps the U.S. That is why America gives Israel $2.6 billion in aid each year. In return, the U.S. gets one of the world's best-trained armies as an ally in the Middle East. Since Israel has such a strong army, no American soldiers are needed to defend its freedom. In Europe, the U.S. must keep over 300,000 soldiers in countries like West Germany, England, Greece, and Spain. This is very expensive. So while $2.6 billion sounds like a lot of money, it is far less than the U.S. spends to defend Europe.

Does the author prove that Israel helps the U.S.? What type of examples does he give?

Israel's strong defenses promote peace in the Middle East. Surrounding Arab nations will not start wars because Israel's army, air force, or navy will respond quickly. Joshua Muravchik, a political expert at the Washington Institute for Near-East Policy, says, "Israel's air and naval forces are the strongest in the eastern Mediterranean." Muravchik also argues that Israel has effectively tested new American planes. By using American fighter jets and modern rockets in their fights with Arab nations, Israel can tell the U.S. how well they work. To U.S. military leaders, this information is priceless. Without it, American fighter pilots might go into battle less prepared.

The author calls Mr. Muravchik a political expert. Does that influence how you interpret his testimonial?

Besides being a military ally, Israel is also a political ally. Israel's constitution is just like that of the United States. It guarantees freedom, human rights, and democracy. By supporting Israel, the U.S. supports democracy in the Middle East. As American author Hyman Bookbinder says, "It is clearly in our nation's interest to be seen by freedom-loving people everywhere as a nation that stands by a friend like Israel."

What propaganda technique is used here? Give reasons for your answer.

America also has a moral duty to stand by Israel. The Jewish nation was created after the Holocaust to protect its citizens from vicious attacks. The U.S. cannot stop giving aid to Israel. Israel cannot survive without it. Since Israel is surrounded by enemies, it needs America's help. If the U.S. abandons Israel, the blood of thousands of innocent citizens would be on its hands.

Words like "abandoned," "blood," and "innocent" often point to what kind of propaganda technique?

Israel can continue only with U.S. aid and support. But it is not a one-way relationship. Israel gives something back to the U.S. While Israel needs the U.S., the U.S. also needs Israel.

The author lists many reasons why the U.S. should support Israel. Name two of them. Is his argument convincing? Why or why not?

Editor's Note: The author of this viewpoint believes that U.S. aid to Israel is harmful. He argues that the aid angers Arab leaders and supports Palestinian oppression.

Why is this a scare tactic?

What image does the word "bully" create? Why do you think the author uses this word?

Israel is no model of democracy. A nation that denies basic human rights to a group of people living within its borders is not a true democracy. Palestinians in the occupied territories cannot vote. They cannot work where they choose. They cannot farm the land of their grandparents. And they cannot protest Israeli rule for fear of injury or death. Fighting for their rights, Palestinians are beaten by Israeli soldiers for breaking curfew, throwing rocks, or distributing PLO literature. The U.S. should not aid such an unjust government.

American aid to Israel is based on the idea that Israel is a weak country in danger of being overrun by its Arab neighbors. The Lebanese war in 1982 and Israel's violent response to the intifada prove this idea wrong. Israel is not weak. It is just the opposite. Israel has become the bully of the Middle East.

Ed Gamble. Reprinted with permission.

America's close tie with Israel offends many countries. Other nations expect America to uphold democracy and freedom. But the U.S. allows Israel to abuse Palestinians, operate deadly raids on neighboring countries, and do business with dictators. Israel makes the U.S. look bad in the world's eyes.

James G. Abourezk writes that Israel sells weapons to anyone with money, including the racist government in South Africa. Abourezk, a former U.S. senator and founder of the American Arab Anti-Discrimination Committee, says that Israel's customers range from communists to dictators. Israel helped the U.S. illegally supply the Nicaraguan contras with weapons in 1986. That incident embarrassed the U.S. government. Without Israel's help, the U.S. would not have gotten into trouble.

What organization does Mr. Abourezk work for? How might that influence his opinion?

Many military experts say Israel provides the U.S. with a strong ally in the Middle East. That argument is flawed. While Israel has a good army, some people question whether Israel would use it to protect American interests. Numerous Israeli leaders have said that Israel's survival is more important than anything else in the world. Cheryl Rubenberg, writing in the Arab newspaper *El-Fajr,* says, "Israel not only does nothing to serve American interests, it repeatedly does things that are harmful to the United States." Israel will always do what is best for Israel, not what is best for the United States. For example, if a large Arab army threatened to cut off the West's oil supply, Israel would not help the U.S. Israel's leaders have proven time and again that survival is their top priority. Helping allies comes second. Aiding Israel does not make America stronger. As a matter of fact, this unholy alliance actually weakens the U.S.

The author says U.S. aid to Israel weakens America. Is this a scare tactic? Why or why not?

U.S. aid to Israel is wasted money. America will remain strong whether or not it continues to support Israel. The U.S. does not need Israel. To promote peace in the Middle East, America must cut its aid to Israel and start helping Arab nations.

Why does the author think aid to Israel is wasted? Who does he think should receive more money, Israel or the Arab nations? After reading these two viewpoints, what do you think the U.S. should do? Give three reasons to support your opinion.

Many speakers and writers quote or paraphrase the ideas of famous people and experts. They usually use these testimonials to add weight to their own argument. It is important to examine testimonials to see if they really do support the argument.

Below are several examples of testimonials. Evaluate each one and mark it according to the following code:

G for good use of a testimonial

P for a poor testimonial—for example, using a celebrity without consideration of his/her knowledge of the topic

I for irrelevant testimonial—one that has nothing to do with the topic under discussion

N for not a testimonial—a quotation that simply provides information and is not intended to add weight to a particular view

EXAMPLE: Journalist Dan Fisher says that 1.4 million Palestinians live in the occupied territories of the West Bank and Gaza Strip.

ANSWER: N—the quote only provides information, it does not present or support an opinion.

Answer

1. The director of Israeli agricultural exports reported that olives were the number one crop in the West Bank in 1989. _____

2. Israeli Prime Minister Yitzhak Shamir says that negotiating with the PLO would harm his government. _____

3. Mona Rishmawi, a Palestinian lawyer who works for a legal rights organization on the West Bank, testifies that Israelis have broken their own laws concerning civil rights. _____

4. An American Jewish actress spoke at a rally protesting Israel's occupation of the territories. She calls for a complete withdrawal of Israeli troops. _____

5. Journalist Anthony Parsons says that the political situation in Israel has changed drastically since the intifada began. _____

6. Arab historian George Antonius writes that Arabs and Jews lived together peacefully in the Middle East for centuries. _____

PREFACE: Is Peace Possible?

On September 17, 1978, three national leaders gained worldwide attention by signing a peace treaty between Egypt and Israel. Egyptian President Anwar Sadat shook hands with Israeli Prime Minister Menachem Begin while U.S. President Jimmy Carter looked on. The agreement, called the Camp David accords, marked the first time any Arab and Israeli leader had made peace. The world hoped that a permanent peace in the Middle East was at last possible. Unfortunately, this would not happen.

In October 1981, Anwar Sadat was assassinated by Moslem radicals within his own army. These radicals had never forgiven Sadat for making peace with Israel. Since then, few Arab leaders have been willing to risk negotiating with Israel. Leaders on both sides of the Arab/Israeli conflict fear the extremists within their movements.

Some people question, for these reasons and others, whether or not peace will ever come to Israel. The following viewpoints give very different opinions on this issue.

Editor's Note: Many political commentators have little hope that peace will come soon to the Middle East. The author of this viewpoint disagrees. He and the people whose testimonials he uses believe that steps toward peace are already being taken.

The author compares Israel to Eastern Europe and South Africa. Is this a good comparison? Why or why not?

Saying the U.S. is responsible for the bloodshed is what propaganda technique?

A new era in world politics is sweeping the globe. Communism has fallen in Eastern Europe. Nelson Mandela and the African National Congress are free in South Africa. Fighting between Iran and Iraq has stopped. If these earth-shattering events can take place, surely peace can come to the Arabs and Israelis.

The U.S. can help speed this process. Just as former President Jimmy Carter helped patch the wounds between Egypt and Israel, so too can the current U.S. administration bring together the suffering Palestinians and the weary Israelis. If U.S. leaders do not help promote peace, they too will be responsible for the Palestinian and Israeli lives lost in the ongoing violent protests.

Steve Kelley. Copley News Service. Reprinted with permission.

Even the PLO, once a hated and feared terrorist group, has given up violence until a peaceful solution can be reached. At one time, the PLO refused to even recognize the right of Israel to exist. Now the PLO is willing to let Israel live in peace if the Palestinians receive a homeland. Rami Khouri, Palestinian writer and editor for the *Jordan Times,* writes, "For the first time since 1948, the Arab world is talking in terms of a negotiated, peaceful and permanent resolution of the conflict with Israel." Khouri argues that both sides must act quickly or the possibility for peace will vanish.

Is this a good use of a testimonial? Why or why not?

Like the Palestinians, Israelis are becoming more moderate. They now show a willingness to negotiate. Most Israelis believe their government should return some or all of the occupied territories to the Palestinians. They realize that an independent Palestinian state is the only path to a lasting peace.

All Israelis and Palestinians, regardless of their politics, are tired of the bloodshed. The endless strikes and curfews cost Palestinians millions of dollars per year. Their families are torn apart by the beatings, jailings, and death. They cannot hold out forever. Likewise, the Israelis suffer. The intifada hurts their weak economy. Buses are burned. Innocent bystanders are hit by rocks. Soldiers are forced to chase children, beat rock throwers, and face screaming Arab mothers. No one enjoys it. Both Palestinians and Israelis realize that the madness cannot continue.

Are these descriptions of violence informative?

Is this a scare tactic? Why or why not?

In this time when the face of world politics is changing, there remains hope that peace will come to Israel. It is possible. Yehoshafat Harkabi, the former head of Israeli Defense Forces Intelligence, is hopeful. He writes, "Israel faces a moment of truth. . . . Let us begin to think about our situation seriously. I am still optimistic about the possibility of an agreement." If a man at the head of the Israeli army can have hope, others should too.

Mr. Harkabi has access to secret information. Does that make his testimonial more important? Why or why not?

Despite years of violence, the author has hope that peace will come to Israel. He argues that both Palestinians and Israelis are becoming more moderate. What evidence does he give to support this argument? Do you agree with the author? Why or why not?

Editor's Note: The author of this viewpoint writes that Israel has always been a battleground. He sees no hope that this history of constant fighting will change. Note the propaganda techniques the author uses to support his opinion.

The word "fool" stands out. Is this a propaganda technique? Why or why not?

Anyone who believes peace will come to Arabs and Israelis is a fool. The conflicting Jewish and Palestinian claims to the land make peace impossible. History teaches us that the land of Israel has been a battleground for centuries. The future will be no different.

The issue of who should live in Israel cannot be discussed without emotion. Orthodox Jews believe God promised the land to their ancestors thousands of years ago. They do not care that Palestinians have farmed the land for seven centuries. To Orthodox Jews, fulfilling God's will is more important than world opinion or international law. How can anyone hope to negotiate with people like this?

BY GAMBLE FOR THE FLORIDA TIMES-UNION, JACKSONVILLE

Ed Gamble. Reprinted with permission.

Most Israeli Jews agree that Israel must give up land to the Palestinians to achieve peace. These moderates are not the problem. People like writer Mordechai Nisan are the problem. In the *Jerusalem Post* he writes, "It is nowhere provided that non-Jews will enjoy full equal rights as a national community. After all, the Land is the eternal possession of the Jewish people alone." For Israelis like Nisan, there can be no compromise.

On the Arab side, the situation is no better. While many moderates would accept the West Bank and Gaza Strip as a homeland, extremists will not rest until Israel is wiped out. David Bar-Illan writes, "What makes Israel's situation truly bad is that 300 million Arabs consider the very existence of Israel an offense to their sense of history and destiny." Bar-Illan is the director of the Jonathan Institute, an anti-terrorist foundation. He thinks that even if Israel gives Palestinians a homeland, it will not bring peace. Bar-Illan says the PLO would simply launch terrorist attacks from its new country into Israel.

The long history of fighting between Arab and Jew will continue. Their dual claims to the same land make peace impossible. Nothing anybody does will change this situation. The hopelessness of the situation is summed up by the attitude of Meir Kahane, founder of the right-wing Kach party in Israel. "I feel no guilt over the fact that I believe *and know* that the Land of Israel is the exclusive home of the Jewish people and that no other people has the slightest right to it."

Do you think Mr. Nisan is Arab or Jewish? How might that affect his opinion?

Mr. Bar-Illan's argument is frightening. Does his job influence his opinion?

The author holds no hope for peace in the Middle East. Is this a scare tactic? Why not?

The author believes peace is not possible. What reasons does he give? How does this viewpoint contrast with the previous viewpoint? List two pairs of opposing testimonials from each viewpoint. Which testimonials offer more information? How does this affect your opinion toward this topic?

4 Understanding Editorial Cartoons

Throughout this book, you have seen cartoons that illustrate the ideas in the viewpoints. Editorial cartoons are an effective and usually humorous way of presenting an opinion on an issue. Cartoonists, like writers, can use ways of persuading you that include deceptive techniques. While many cartoons are easy to understand, others may require more thought.

The cartoon below is similar to cartoons that appear in your daily newspaper. It emphasizes a point made in Viewpoint 8 stating that peace between Arabs and Israelis is impossible. Look at the cartoon. How does it illustrate that point?

Paul Conrad, © 1989, Los Angeles Times. Reprinted with permission.

What is the cartoonist's opinion of Israel's role in the peace talks? How can you tell? Do you agree with the cartoonist's opinion? Why or why not?